Good Catch, SNOOPY!

by Charles M. Schulz

Selected Cartoons from
BIG LEAGUE PEANUTS
Volume 2

FAWCETT CREST • NEW YORK

A Fawcett Crest Book
Published by Ballantine Books
Contents of Book: PEANUTS® Comic Strips by Charles M. Schulz

Published in the United States by Ballantine Books, a division of Random House, Inc., New York and simultaneously in Canada by Random House of Canada Limited, Toronto.

Library of Congress Catalog Card Number: 85-60951

ISBN 0-449-21291-2

This book comprises a portion of BIG LEAGUE PEANUTS and is reprinted by arrangement with Henry Holt and Company.

Manufactured in the United States of America

First Ballantine Books Edition: July 1987

10 9 8 7 6 5 4 3 2 1

Good Catch, SNOOPY!

HEY MANAGER, WE CAN'T LOSE TODAY...

SEE? I HAVE GLOVES ON BOTH HANDS AND BOTH FEET!

THAT'S GREAT! HERE'S ANOTHER ONE THAT MIGHT HELP...

SCHULZ

THEY TOLD ME I HAVE A CUTE STRIKE ZONE!

SCHULZ

BONK

NO PROBLEM, MANAGER.. I MISSED IT, BUT THE GROUND CAUGHT IT!

NICE CATCH, GROUND! YOU'RE DOING A GOOD JOB!

I NEVER REALIZED THE GROUND WAS ON OUR SIDE...
SCHULZ

I DON'T KNOW WHY I EVEN KEEP YOU ON OUR TEAM...

I HAVE BOX OFFICE APPEAL, THAT'S WHY!

WE DON'T **HAVE** A BOX OFFICE!

IF YOU EVER GET A BOX OFFICE, I BET I'LL APPEAL TO IT!!
SCHULZ

HERE..HAVE A DOUGHNUT..
THANK YOU..

I WONDER HOW CHARLIE BROWN EVER GOT TO BE OUR MANAGER..NONE OF US HAS ANY RESPECT FOR HIM..
MANAGER

I SUPPOSE IT'S A MATTER OF DEDICATION..

CHARLIE BROWN IS THE ONLY ONE WHO IS COMPLETELY DEDICATED TO BASEBALL..THIS IS WHAT MAKES A GOOD MANAGER..

I THINK HE'D RATHER MANAGE THAN EAT
HERE, CHARLIE BROWN.. HAVE A DOUGHNUT..
NO, THANK YOU.. I'D RATHER MANAGE!
MANAGER

YOU'RE RIGHT!
SCHULZ

THE FIRST BATTER HIT ONE OVER MY HEAD...

THE SECOND BATTER HIT ONE IN FRONT OF ME..

THE THIRD BATTER HIT ONE TO MY LEFT AND THE FOURTH BATTER HIT ONE TO MY RIGHT...

I'M LOOKING FORWARD TO THIS NEXT BATTER!
SCHULZ

I'VE BEEN GOING OVER OUR BASEBALL STATISTICS FOR THIS PAST YEAR..
WHEN I THINK OF ALL THOSE GAMES WE LOST, I GET SICK..
WINNING ISN'T EVERYTHING, CHARLIE BROWN...
THAT'S TRUE, BUT LOSING ISN'T ANYTHING!
SCHULZ

HEY, MANAGER, HOLD IT A MINUTE!

AS LONG AS I HAVE TO STAND IN THE OUTFIELD, I THOUGHT I MIGHT AS WELL GO BAREFOOTED...KEEP AN EYE ON MY SHOES FOR ME, WILL YOU?

MAYBE YOU WANT ME TO HAVE THEM BRONZED!!

WHAT A SARCASTIC MANAGER!

IN CASE YOU DIDN'T KNOW, THE BALL DOESN'T HAVE TO STOP ROLLING BEFORE YOU CAN PICK IT UP!!

IT WAS HAVING A GOOD TIME, AND I DIDN'T WANT TO DISTURB IT
SCHULZ

CRACK!

CLOMP!
IN APPRECIATION OF THE GREAT PLAY YOU MADE THIS AFTERNOON, SNOOPY, THE TEAM HAS ASKED ME TO PRESENT YOU THIS...
HOW NICE... THE "GOLDEN MOUTH" AWARD!
SCHULZ

GOOD GRIEF! IT'S MORNING ALREADY!
THIS IS THE DAY OF OUR FIRST GAME

I'M NO MANAGER...I CAN'T RUN A BASEBALL TEAM...EVERYBODY KNOWS I'M A LOUSY MANAGER... NOBODY EVEN PAYS ANY ATTENTION TO ME...THEY ALL HATE ME...

I THINK I'LL JUST STAY IN BED... MAYBE IT'LL RAIN...MAYBE NO ONE ELSE WILL SHOW UP EITHER.. I'LL JUST STAY IN BED, AND...

OKAY, MANAGER! RISE, AND SHINE!
SCHULZ

GET OUT! GET WAY OUT!!
LET'S TRY TO GET IN ON THOSE!
SCHULZ

MY DAD TOOK ME TO A BALL GAME YESTERDAY, CHARLIE BROWN..

THEY HAD A REAL DUGOUT, AND A WATER COOLER, AND A BAT RACK AND A DRESSING ROOM.. WE DON'T HAVE ANY OF THOSE THINGS!

DID YOU NOTICE SOMETHING ELSE THAT THEY HAD?
WHAT'S THAT?

REAL PLAYERS!
SCHULZ

HEY, MANAGER, IT'S HOT OUT THERE IN CENTER FIELD

WOULD YOU CARE IF I PUT ON MY BIKINI ? AND AS LONG AS I HAD ON MY BIKINI, WOULD YOU CARE IF I WENT TO THE BEACH ? AND AS LONG AS I'M AT THE BEACH, WOULD YOU CARE IF I JUST FORGOT ABOUT THE BALL GAME ?

GET BACK OUT THERE IN CENTER FIELD WHERE YOU BELONG!

YOU'D THINK A MANAGER WOULD APPRECIATE AN OUTFIELDER WHO LOOKED GOOD IN A BIKINI....
SCHULZ

WHAT'S THIS TREE DOING HERE?!

I PLANTED IT FOR YOU, MANAGER..

NOW, AFTER YOU LOSE A GAME, YOU WON'T HAVE TO WALK SO FAR TO BANG YOUR HEAD AGAINST A TREE

IT'LL EVEN BE SO CONVENIENT, THAT YOU'LL BE ABLE TO BANG YOUR HEAD AGAINST IT AFTER EVERY INNING!

GET THAT TREE OUT OF HERE!

I'LL CALL BILLY MARTIN.. MAYBE HE'LL WANT IT...
SCHULZ

LUCY! WAKE UP!
Z

HOW CAN YOU FALL ASLEEP IN THE MIDDLE OF A BALL GAME?

SORRY, MANAGER... WATCHING YOUR GRACEFUL MOVES ON THE PITCHER'S MOUND LULLED ME TO SLEEP!

YES, I CAN SEE HOW THAT MIGHT HAPPEN...
SCHULZ

YOU THINK YOU'D BE HAPPY IF YOU WON A BALL GAME, DON'T YOU, CHARLIE BROWN?
THE DOCTOR IS IN

WELL, YOU WOULDN'T! IF YOU WON ONE GAME, YOU'D WANT TO WIN ANOTHER, AND THEN ANOTHER!

SOON YOU'D WANT TO WIN EVERY BALL GAME YOU PLAYED...

YEAHHH!!
SCHULZ

JOE DI MAGGIO NEVER COMPLAINED ABOUT PLAYING BALL ON A HOT DAY!
WHO WAS JOE DI MAGGIO?
ONE OF THE GREATEST OUTFIELDERS WHO EVER LIVED, THAT'S WHO!
I THOUGHT HE JUST DRANK COFFEE
SCHULZ

WELL, OL' FAITHFUL GLOVE, ANOTHER SEASON HAS COME AND GONE... I GUESS I'LL PUT YOU AWAY UNTIL NEXT SPRING...
SIGH THERE I WAS, A BEAUTIFUL PIECE OF GENUINE LEATHER...
SO WHAT HAPPENS? I END UP AS A BASEBALL GLOVE FOR A STUPID KID WHO LOSES EVERY GAME HE PITCHES!
OF COURSE, IT MIGHT HAVE BEEN WORSE... I COULD HAVE BEEN A PAIR OF GOALIE PADS AND GOT HIT BY PUCKS ALL WINTER...
SCHULZ

LAST YEAR OUR TEAM LACKED POWER..
THEREFORE, THE FIRST THING I WANT YOU TO DO TODAY IS PRACTICE YOUR HITTING

BONK!
LET ME WORD THAT A LITTLE DIFFERENTLY...

I SEE WE HAVE A CAPACITY CROWD TODAY, CHARLIE BROWN

YES, I NOTICED THAT, TOO...

THE SEAT IS JAMMED
SCHULZ

ONE FINGER WILL MEAN A STRAIGHT BALL, TWO FINGERS WILL MEAN A STRAIGHT BALL, THREE FINGERS WILL MEAN A STRAIGHT BALL AND FOUR FINGERS WILL MEAN A STRAIGHT BALL...
I HAVE A VERY SARCASTIC CATCHER
SCHULZ

HEY, MANAGER, MY GLOVE IS SO STIFF I CAN'T CATCH THE BALL!
THAT'S BECAUSE YOU HAVEN'T USED IT ALL WINTER...TRY RUBBING A LITTLE NEAT'S-FOOT OIL INTO IT
FORGET IT!
I HATE ANY SPORT WHERE YOU HAVE TO TAKE CARE OF YOUR EQUIPMENT!
SCHULZ

WUMP!

KLUNK

BUMP!

TAKE OFF THOSE STUPID GLASSES!!!

MAKE A GUY A MANAGER, AND RIGHT AWAY HE TURNS INTO A CRABBY OLD MAN!
SCHULZ

WELL, WE LOST AGAIN
WE WON A MORAL VICTORY, THOUGH, DIDN'T WE?

NO, WE DIDN'T EVEN WIN A MORAL VICTORY
WE DIDN'T?
I HATE IT WHEN WE DON'T EVEN WIN A MORAL VICTORY
SCHULZ

HEY, MANAGER, YOU SHOULD READ THIS BOOK

IT'S CALLED, "WINNING AND TEN OTHER CHOICES"

WHAT ARE THE TEN OTHER CHOICES?

TYING, LOSING, LOSING, LOSING, LOSING, LOSING, LOSING, LOSING, LOSING AND LOSING!
SCHULZ

I'VE BEEN THINKING ABOUT SOMETHING...
IN THE BIG LEAGUES, WHEN A TEAM GETS A RALLY STARTED, SOMEONE BLOWS A TRUMPET AND EVERYONE YELLS, "CHARGE!!"
DO YOU THINK WE COULD DO THAT, CHARLIE BROWN?
I DON'T KNOW...WE'VE NEVER HAD A RALLY...
SCHULZ

DID YOU SEE HOW I STRUCK OUT THAT LAST KID? PRETTY GOOD PITCHING, HUH?
YEAH, THAT WAS THAT KID WHO'S BEEN SICK IN BED ALL WINTER..HIS DOCTOR SAYS HE'S GOING TO BE ALL RIGHT, BUT TO GET OUT IN THE SUN...
HE ALSO DOESN'T SEE VERY WELL, AND HE'S NEVER PLAYED BASEBALL BEFORE...

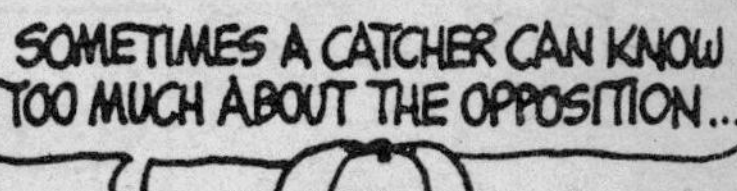
SOMETIMES A CATCHER CAN KNOW TOO MUCH ABOUT THE OPPOSITION...

SCHULZ

AHEM!

DON'T TELL ME YOU'RE THINKING ABOUT EATING AT A TIME LIKE THIS? ARE YOU OUT OF YOUR MIND?

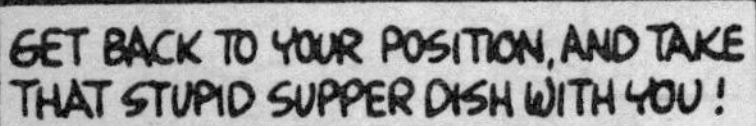
GET BACK TO YOUR POSITION, AND TAKE THAT STUPID SUPPER DISH WITH YOU!

!

AND PAY ATTENTION TO THE BALL GAME!

PLUNK

PTUI!

I SUPPOSE IT WOULDN'T HURT TO LET HIM HAVE A LITTLE SNACK BETWEEN INNINGS...
SCHULZ

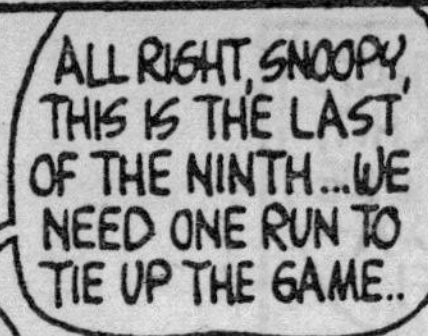
ALL RIGHT, SNOOPY, THIS IS THE LAST OF THE NINTH...WE NEED ONE RUN TO TIE UP THE GAME..

I WANT YOU TO GO UP THERE WITH TEETH-GRITTING DETERMINATION, AND GET ON BASE! LET'S SEE YOU GRIT YOUR TEETH...

THAT'S FINE...KEEP GRITTING YOUR TEETH, AND YOU'LL GET A HIT!

I FEEL LIKE A FOOL...
SCHULZ

LOOK AT THAT! LINUS GOT A HIT, TOO! I KNEW WE STILL HAD A CHANCE!

IF YOU GRIT YOUR TEETH, AND SHOW REAL DETERMINATION, YOU ALWAYS HAVE A CHANCE! YOU'RE UP NEXT, LUCY...LET'S SEE YOU GRIT YOUR TEETH...

FANTASTIC! YOU'LL SCARE THEIR PITCHER TO DEATH! KEEP GRITTING YOUR TEETH, AND GO GET A HIT!

GET A HIT?! I CAN'T EVEN SEE WHERE I'M GOING..
SCHULZ

STRIKE ONE!

OOOOOO! C'MON, CHARLIE BROWN, HIT IT! FOR ONCE IN YOUR LIFE, HIT IT!!

WOULDN'T YOU LIKE JUST FOR ONCE TO SEE CHARLIE BROWN HIT THAT BALL?
NO..

I'M NOT PREPARED TO HAVE THE WORLD COME TO AN END!
SCHULZ

STRIKE TWO!

NOW, I'M GOING TO GRIT MY TEETH, AND BEAR DOWN! IF A PERSON GRITS HIS TEETH, AND SHOWS REAL DETERMINATION, HE CAN'T FAIL!

STRIKE THREE!

YOU BLOCKHEAD!
SCHULZ

YOUR TROUBLE, CHARLIE BROWN, IS THAT YOU LIVE BY MOTTOS AND TRITE SAYINGS..
YOU REALLY THOUGHT THAT IF YOU GRITTED YOUR TEETH IT WOULD HELP YOU TO BECOME A HERO.. WELL, THERE'S MORE TO LIFE THAN JUST GRITTING YOUR TEETH...

CHARLIE BROWN, DO YOU UNDERSTAND WHAT I'M TRYING TO TELL YOU?
MAYBE I DIDN'T GRIT THEM HARD ENOUGH...MAYBE IF I...
SIGH!
SCHULZ

WHAT ARE YOU DOING, CHARLIE BROWN?
I'M TRYING TO FIGURE OUT MY PITCHING RECORD FOR THIS YEAR..

YOU TAKE THE NUMBER OF EARNED RUNS, AND MULTIPLY BY NINE AND THEN DIVIDE BY THE NUMBER OF INNINGS PITCHED

WHAT DID YOU GET?

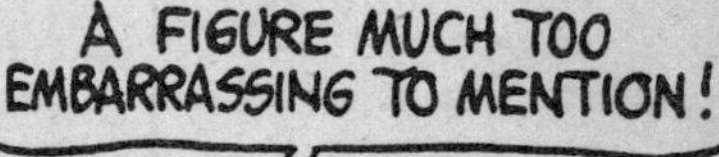
A FIGURE MUCH TOO EMBARRASSING TO MENTION!

SCHULZ

BONK!

AAUGH!

LUCY! HOW COULD YOU MISS THAT BALL?! IT CAME RIGHT TO YOU! HOW COULD YOU MISS IT?!!

I NEVER THINK ABOUT THE PAST
SCHULZ

HEY, MANAGER, ARE WE SUPPOSED TO YELL, "I GOT IT!" OR "I HAVE IT!"?

IT DOESN'T MATTER, LUCY

I THINK HE'S RIGHT
KLUNK!

IF YOU DON'T GOT IT, YOU DON'T HAVE IT!
SCHULZ

LOST AGAIN! I CAN'T STAND IT!

WHY CAN'T WE EVER **WIN**?

WHY? WHY? WHY?

BECAUSE WE'RE NO GOOD... BECAUSE WE'RE NO GOOD... BECAUSE WE'RE NO GOOD!
SCHULZ

NEXT YEAR I'M GONNA BE A FREE AGENT
YOU ARE, HUH?
DO YOU KNOW WHAT A FREE AGENT IS?
NOPE

BUT I'M GONNA BE ONE!!
SCHULZ

OKAY, LUCY, WHERE WERE YOU ON THAT FLY BALL? LET'S START PAYING ATTENTION!

BLEAH!

AND HOW ABOUT YOU? YOU WERE OUT OF POSITION ON THAT DOUBLE-PLAY BALL! YOU BETTER LOOK ALIVE!

BLEAH!

AND YOU SURE HAVEN'T BEEN DOING MUCH OF A JOB BEHIND THE PLATE, SCHROEDER! HOW ABOUT SHOWING SOME LIFE BACK THERE, HUH? HOW ABOUT IT?

BLEAH!

MAYBE I WAS TOO HARD ON THEM...AFTER ALL, I HAVEN'T BEEN DOING TOO WELL MYSELF...IN FACT, MY PITCHING HAS BEEN LOUSY!

BY GOLLY, CHARLIE BROWN, YOU'D BETTER START PITCHING BETTER BALL!! YOU'D BETTER BUCKLE DOWN OUT HERE!

BLEAH!
SCHULZ

WHAT'RE YOU GUYS TALKING ABOUT?

WE'RE TRYING TO FIGURE OUT SOME STRATEGY
HOW ABOUT TRYING A SQUEEZE PLAY?

A SQUEEZE PLAY?!

I'LL SQUEEZE THE CATCHER!
!
SCHULZ

LOOK, IF YOU DON'T STOP BOTHERING MY CATCHER, HE'S GOING TO QUIT THE TEAM!

I JUST WANT TO GIVE HIM A LITTLE KISS...
WELL, KISS SOMEONE ELSE! THERE ARE SEVEN OTHER GUYS ON THE TEAM YOU CAN KISS!

ALL RIGHT, SIX OTHER GUYS!
SCHULZ

POW!

WELL, THAT DOES IT FOR ANOTHER SEASON, MANAGER! NOW, YOU HAVE TWO CHOICES..

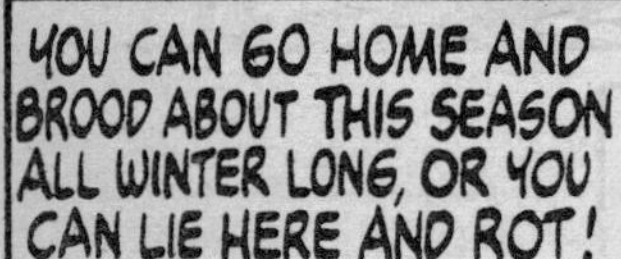
YOU CAN GO HOME AND BROOD ABOUT THIS SEASON ALL WINTER LONG, OR YOU CAN LIE HERE AND ROT!

THOSE ARE GREAT CHOICES
SCHULZ

I'M GLAD THE BASEBALL SEASON IS OVER FOR US!

I DON'T EVEN WANT TO HEAR THE WORD 'BASEBALL' ANY MORE! I THINK IF I HEAR THE WORD 'BASEBALL' AGAIN, I'LL SCREAM!

BASEBALL

AAUGH!
SCHULZ

SEE THIS FIVE DOLLARS? I'M GOING TO SPEND IT ALL ON BUBBLE GUM CARDS! I'VE **GOT** TO GET A PICTURE OF **JOE SHLABOTNIK**!

FIVE DOLLARS' WORTH OF BUBBLE GUM, PLEASE!

I'D DO ANYTHING TO GET A JOE SHLABOTNIK BUBBLE GUM CARD.. HE'S MY HERO...

FIVE DOLLARS' WORTH OF BUBBLE GUM, AND NOT ONE JOE SHLABOTNIK!

A PENNY'S WORTH OF BUBBLE GUM, PLEASE..

WELL, WHAT DO YOU KNOW...JOE SHLABOTNIK!
SCHULZ

RATS! WE LOST THE FIRST GAME OF THE SEASON AGAIN!
LOSING A BALL GAME IS LIKE DROPPING AN ICE CREAM CONE ON THE SIDEWALK...
IT JUST LAYS THERE, AND YOU KNOW YOU'VE DROPPED IT AND THERE'S NOTHING YOU CAN DO.... IT'S TOO LATE....
RATS!
SCHULZ

DID YOU FEEL AS BAD ABOUT LOSING OUR FIRST GAME AS I DID, LUCY?

OH, YES, CHARLIE BROWN... I SAT UP ALL NIGHT CRYING MY EYES OUT!

HAHAHAHAHA

NO JURY WOULD EVER CONVICT ME!
SCHULZ

PITCH IT IN THERE, CHARLIE BROWN!

LET'S GET RID OF THESE GUYS ONE, TWO, THREE!
TWO, THREE, FOUR?
SCHULZ

I'M WORKING ON OUR BASEBALL SCHEDULE FOR NEXT SEASON
GET US SOME GAMES WITH SOME REAL LITTLE KIDS, CHARLIE BROWN, SO WE CAN SLAUGHTER THEM...
AND THEN GET US SOME GAMES WITH SOME REAL OLD LADIES, AND WE'LL SLAUGHTER THEM, TOO!
PLAN OUR SCHEDULE RIGHT, CHARLIE BROWN, AND WE'LL HAVE A GREAT SEASON!
SCHULZ

THERE ARE A LOT OF TROUBLES IN THE WORLD TODAY...
PLAYING BASEBALL HELPS TO TAKE YOUR MIND OFF THEM
POW!
I THINK I'D RATHER WORRY ABOUT THE TROUBLES IN THE WORLD
SCHULZ

ONE FINGER MEANS A FAST BALL AND TWO FINGERS MEAN A CURVE..
MMM

THREE FINGERS MEAN A DROP AND FOUR FINGERS MEAN A PITCH-OUT...
WHAT IF I FORGET?

DON'T WORRY ABOUT IT...WE ONLY HAVE SIGNALS TO FOOL THE OTHER TEAM INTO THINKING YOU CAN THROW SOMETHING BESIDES A STRAIGHT BALL!

IT'S ALWAYS NICE TO WORK WITH A CATCHER WHO HAS REAL CONFIDENCE IN YOU!
SCHULZ

I CAN'T LOOK!
THE SCORE IS THREE TO TWO IN THE LAST OF THE NINTH!
BUT WE HAVE TWO OUTS!
BUT CHARLIE BROWN IS ON THIRD! AND OUR BEST HITTER IS COMING UP!

SAY, YOU DON'T THINK CHARLIE BROWN WILL TRY TO STEAL HOME, DO YOU?
NEVER! NOT EVEN CHARLIE BROWN WOULD DO ANYTHING THAT STUPID!
I WONDER IF I SHOULD TRY TO STEAL HOME !?
SCHULZ

THIS IS MY BIG CHANCE TO BE A **HERO**!
IF I COULD STEAL HOME, THE GAME WOULD BE ALL TIED UP, AND **I'D** BE THE **HERO**!

SCHULZ
I HAVEN'T GOT THE NERVE!

I'M GONNA STEAL HOME, AND I'M GONNA BE A HERO!

GET READY NOW....HERE I GO...DON'T BE A COWARD.... HERE I GO...DON'T BE SCARED...

HERE I GO....ZOOM....HERE I GO...DON'T BE A COWARD... HERE I GO...DON'T BE SCARED...

HERE I STAY!

I GOTTA TRY IT!
IF I'M GONNA BE A HERO, I GOTTA TRY TO STEAL HOME!

FIRST I'LL DANCE AROUND A LITTLE ON THE BASELINE TO CONFUSE THEIR PITCHER...

...AND THEN I'LL...

TAKE OFF!
SCHULZ

SLIDE, CHARLIE BROWN! SLIDE!

WHAAAH!
WE LOST THE GAME ALL BECAUSE OF CHARLIE BROWN
WHHAAAAAHHH!!

WAS I OUT?
OUT?! WHY, YOU BLOCKHEAD, YOU DIDN'T EVEN GET HALF WAY HOME!

RATS!
SCHULZ

THIS IS OUR LAST GAME OF THE SEASON, CHARLIE BROWN...LET'S WIN IT!
OKAY, GET OUT THERE AND PLAY YOUR BEST...

YOU ALWAYS HAVE TO SAY SOMETHING SARCASTIC, DON'T YOU?
SCHULZ

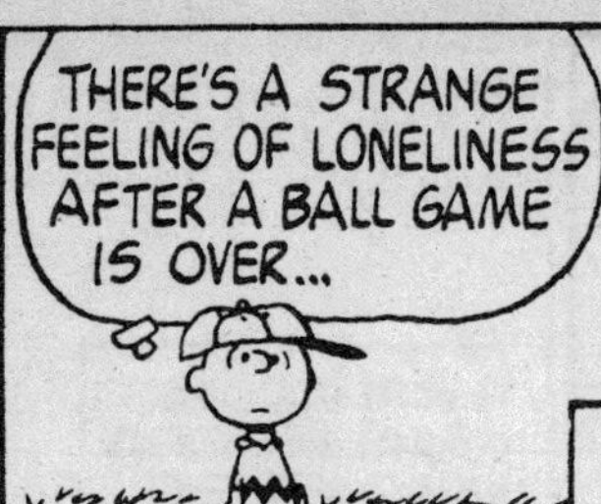
THERE'S A STRANGE FEELING OF LONELINESS AFTER A BALL GAME IS OVER...

THE FIELD IS EMPTY... THE AIR IS SILENT... THE SHADOWS BEGIN TO LENGTHEN...

SOON NOTHING IS LEFT BUT MEMORIES

STUPID KID... I DIDN'T THINK HE WAS EVER GOING TO LEAVE!
SCHULZ

I MISS THE BASEBALL SEASON...

I MISS STANDING OUT HERE ON THE PITCHER'S MOUND WITH THE EXCITEMENT OF THE GAME ALL AROUND ME..

LADIES AND GENTLEMEN, THE LINEUPS FOR TODAY'S GAME...

INDULGING IN A LITTLE FANTASY, EH, CHARLIE BROWN? OKAY, LET'S PRETEND I'M THE CATCHER...

ALL RIGHT, PITCHER...WE'VE GOT TO GET OUR SIGNALS STRAIGHT....ONE FINGER WILL MEAN A FAST BALL, TWO FINGERS WILL MEAN A CURVE AND YOU KNOW WHAT THREE FINGERS WILL MEAN?

THREE FINGERS WILL MEAN A SNOWBALL! HA! HA! HA! HA! HA!

HER KIND KNOWS NO SEASON!
SCHULZ

RATS! ANOTHER GAME LOST!
I REALLY THOUGHT WE WERE GOING TO WIN THIS ONE...
FOR ONE BRIEF MOMENT VICTORY WAS WITHIN OUR GRASP!
AND THEN THE GAME STARTED!
SCHULZ

THAT'S WHAT IS KNOWN AS
A SPECTACULAR CATCH
OF A ROUTINE FLY BALL!

AAUGH! A SPIDER!!

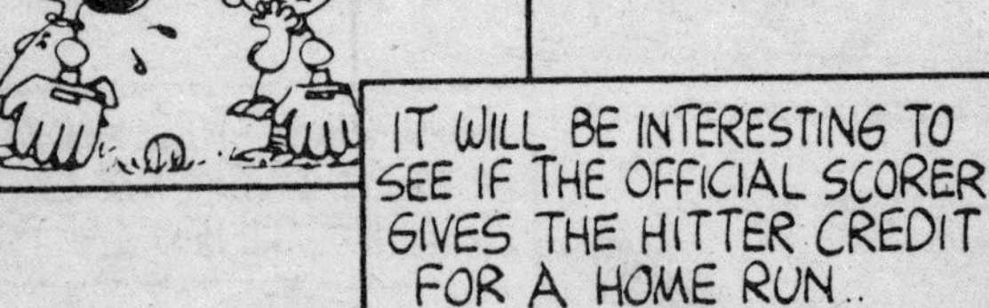
THERE'S A SPIDER ON THE BALL! WE CAN'T PICK UP THE BALL, CHARLIE BROWN! THERE'S A SPIDER ON IT!

IT WILL BE INTERESTING TO SEE IF THE OFFICIAL SCORER GIVES THE HITTER CREDIT FOR A HOME RUN..
SCHULZ

KLOP!
I WONDER WHY HE WEARS A GLOVE...
WHERE ELSE WOULD I KEEP MY LUNCH?
SCHULZ

ALL THEY HAVE TO GO BY IS THE WAY WE WAVE OUR ARMS

SEE, I POINT TO THE OUTFIELD, AND THEY THINK I'M TALKING ABOUT SOMETHING OUT THERE...

NO ONE IN THE STANDS CAN TELL WHAT I'M REALLY SAYING...

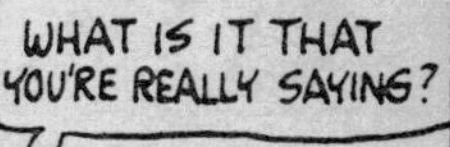
WHAT IS IT THAT YOU'RE REALLY SAYING?

I THINK YOU'RE KIND OF CUTE!

I CAN'T STAND IT!
SIGH
♪
SCHULZ

LET 'IM HIT IT, PITCHER! GO AHEAD, LET 'IM HIT IT!

WE'RE RIGHT BEHIND YOU, PITCHER! LET 'IM HIT IT!

BONK!

I THOUGHT YOU SAID TO LET HIM HIT IT !?!

I DIDN'T THINK YOU EVER LISTENED..
SCHULZ

HEY, MANAGER! I'M MAKING OUT OUR LINEUP...SEE WHAT YOU THINK..

I'VE GOT SCHROEDER DOWN FOR CATCHER, LINUS AT SECOND BASE AND SNOOPY AT SHORTSTOP...

HOW ABOUT DH? WHO'S OUR DESIGNATED HITTER?
I PUT DOWN SHERMY, OKAY?

THAT'S FINE...SHERMY'S A GOOD HITTER
AND I'VE PUT YOU DOWN FOR DG

DG?

DESIGNATED GOAT!
SCHULZ

HEY, MANAGER, WHAT DO THEY MEAN WHEN THEY SAY, "JUST WAIT 'TIL NEXT YEAR"?

THEY MEAN THAT ALTHOUGH THEIR TEAM WASN'T VERY GOOD THIS YEAR, NEXT YEAR THEY'RE GOING TO BE BETTER

JUST WAIT 'TIL TWENTY YEARS FROM NOW!
SCHULZ

I DON'T SUPPOSE YOU'D LET YOURSELF GET HIT ON THE HEAD WITH THE BALL, WOULD YOU ?

THIS IS THE FIRST TIME I'VE EVER LOOKED DIRECTLY INTO THE EYES OF SOMEONE WHO IS TOTALLY OUT OF HIS MIND!

HEY, MANAGER..

NOW WHAT?

I THINK YOUR DOG IS
AFRAID OF THUNDER

BONK

WHAT HAPPENED?
CHARLIE BROWN GOT HIT WITH A LINE-DRIVE!

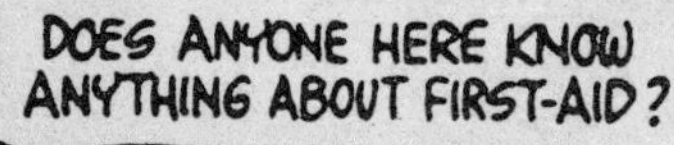
DOES ANYONE HERE KNOW ANYTHING ABOUT FIRST-AID?

IT'S PROBABLY NOT SERIOUS.. SECOND OR THIRD-AID WILL DO

I HATE IT WHEN THE BASEBALL SEASON IS OVER

THERE'S A DREARINESS IN THE AIR THAT DEPRESSES ME...

EVERYTHING SEEMS SAD...EVEN THE OL' PITCHER'S MOUND IS COVERED WITH WEEDS...

I GUESS ALL A PERSON CAN DO IS DREAM HIS DREAMS...MAYBE I'LL BE A GOOD BALL PLAYER SOMEDAY...MAYBE I'LL EVEN PLAY IN THE WORLD SERIES, AND BE A HERO...

?
I BET I WILL PLAY IN THE WORLD SERIES SOMEDAY...I BET I'LL...

HEY! LOOK WHO'S OUT HERE TALKING TO HIMSELF!

WHAT ARE YOU DOING, CHARLIE BROWN, THINKING ABOUT ALL THE TIMES YOU STRUCK OUT?!

THERE'S A DREARINESS IN THE AIR THAT DEPRESSES ME!
SCHULZ

SHOW THIS GUY SOMETHING SPECIAL, CHARLIE BROWN!

GIVE 'IM THE OL' MEMORIAL DAY PITCH!

WHAT'S THE OL' MEMORIAL DAY PITCH ?

I DON'T KNOW...IT JUST SOUNDED GOOD!
SCHULZ

RATS!

WHAT COULD BE WORSE THAN THE LONG WALK HOME AFTER LOSING THE FIRST GAME OF THE SEASON?

HOLD IT A MINUTE, CHARLIE BROWN!

?

YOU WERE WRONG! I TOLD YOU YOU WERE WRONG!!

I TOLD FRIEDA SHE WAS WRONG, BUT SHE WOULDN'T BELIEVE ME...

SHE SAID YOU COULD SEE THE OCEAN FROM UP HERE, BUT I KNEW YOU COULDN'T..

I'M GLAD MY OUTFIELDERS HAVE SUCH INTERESTING DISCUSSIONS!
SCHULZ

THAT LITTLE RED-HAIRED GIRL HAS COME TO WATCH OUR GAME..
I WONDER IF SHE'S LOOKING AT ME.......
SHE WASN'T LOOKING AT ME...
SCHULZ

WHAT ARE YOU DOING, CHARLIE BROWN? WHY DON'T YOU PITCH?
THAT LITTLE RED-HAIRED GIRL. SHE'S WATCHING THE GAME...
OH, GOOD GRIEF!
THIS IS MY BIG CHANCE TO BE A HERO, AND SHE'S WATCHING!

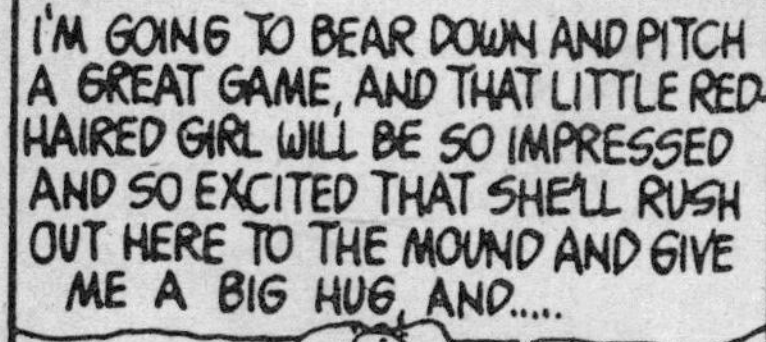
I'M GOING TO BEAR DOWN AND PITCH A GREAT GAME, AND THAT LITTLE RED-HAIRED GIRL WILL BE SO IMPRESSED AND SO EXCITED THAT SHE'LL RUSH OUT HERE TO THE MOUND AND GIVE ME A BIG HUG, AND.....

OH, BROTHER! WHY DO I THINK ABOUT THINGS LIKE THAT?
SCHULZ

GOOD GRIEF, CHARLIE BROWN, WHEN ARE YOU GOING TO THROW THE FIRST PITCH?
THAT LITTLE RED-HAIRED GIRL IS WATCHING... I CAN'T LET GO OF THE BALL.. MY FINGERS ARE NUMB
I'M STARTING TO SHAKE.. LOOK AT ME! I'M SHAKING ALL OVER!
I DON'T SUPPOSE THERE'S A NEUROLOGIST IN THE STANDS..
WOULDN'T A GENERAL PRACTITIONER DO?
HOW ABOUT A VET?

COME ON, CHARLIE BROWN..WE'LL TAKE YOU HOME..
I'M GOING TO PITCH A GREAT GAME..

THAT LITTLE RED-HAIRED GIRL IS WATCHING, AND I'M GOING TO PITCH A GREAT GAME, AND SHE'S GOING TO BE IMPRESSED, AND...

WE'LL TAKE YOU HOME, CHARLIE BROWN, AND YOU CAN GO TO BED UNTIL YOU STOP SHAKING...

I'M GOING TO BE THE HERO AND PITCH A GREAT GAME AND THAT LITTLE RED-HAIRED GIRL WILL BE WATCHING AND I'LL BE PITCHING AND I'LL BE GREAT AND SHE'LL BE THERE AN..
SCHULZ

OKAY, START THE GAME!
I FEEL BETTER! I'VE STOPPED SHAKING!
THE GAME'S OVER, CHARLIE BROWN, AND GUESS WHAT... WE WON!

LINUS TOOK YOUR PLACE... HE PITCHED A GREAT GAME... AND THERE WAS THIS LITTLE RED-HAIRED GIRL WATCHING...

SHE GOT SO EXCITED AFTER THE GAME THAT SHE RUSHED OUT TO THE MOUND AND GAVE LINUS A BIG HUG!
AAUGH!
SCHULZ

MY FRIEND
MY FRIEND, THE RELIEF PITCHER

MY FRIEND, THE RELIEF PITCHER, WHO PITCHED A GREAT GAME, AND IMPRESSED THAT LITTLE RED-HAIRED GIRL SO MUCH THAT SHE RAN OUT AND GAVE HIM A BIG HUG!
MY FRIEND!

I WONDER IF IT'S GOING TO BE TOO HOT TO PLAY TODAY...

DON'T WORRY ABOUT THE HEAT, MANAGER..

IF YOU WEAR YOUR CAP UPSIDE DOWN, AND FILL IT WITH ICE WATER, THE HEAT WON'T BOTHER YOU A BIT!

WHAT HAPPENS IF YOU HAVE TO CATCH A HIGH FLY BALL?

YOU'D HAVE TO BE CRAZY TO PLAY BALL ON A DAY LIKE THIS..
SCHULZ

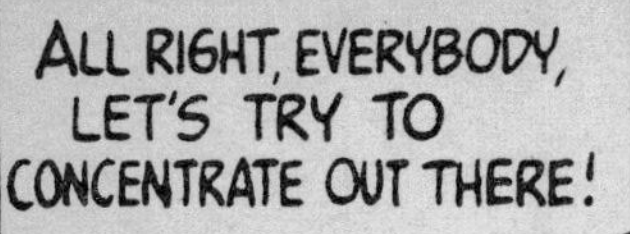
ALL RIGHT, EVERYBODY, LET'S TRY TO CONCENTRATE OUT THERE!

BONK!!

I THOUGHT I TOLD YOU TO CONCENTRATE
I THOUGHT YOU SAID MEDITATE..

THAT'S THE RULE...IF THE BALL ROLLS OVER YOU, YOU GET TO GO TO FIRST BASE...
SCHULZ

LET 'IM HIT IT!
IT'S BORING OUT HERE!

BONK!

BORING IS BETTER

INTERESTING HURTS!

CHARLIE BROWN, I WANT YOU TO KNOW THAT I THINK YOU'RE A GREAT PITCHER!
WHY, THANK YOU, LUCY..THANK YOU VERY MUCH..I APPRECIATE THAT
APRIL FOOL!
I CAN'T STAND IT... I JUST CAN'T STAND IT...
HEE HEE HEE HEE
SCHULZ

RIGHT-FIELD? ARE YOU SURE?
OF COURSE, I'M SURE..
WATCH..
WHAP

PLUNK

ALL RIGHT... WHO YOU GOT DOWN FOR LEFT-FIELD ?
SCHULZ

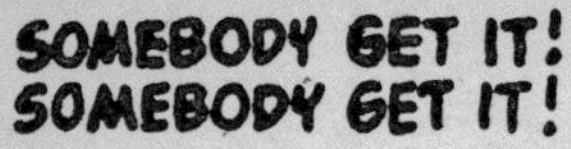
SOMEBODY GET IT! SOMEBODY GET IT!

I GOT IT! I GOT IT!

DON'T SAY YOU'VE GOT IT UNLESS YOU'RE SURE YOU'VE GOT IT!

IN MY HUMBLE OPINION, I THINK I'VE GOT IT...

EIGHTY-SIX TO NOTHING! HOW COULD WE LOSE EIGHTY-SIX TO NOTHING?

I'M SURPRISED THAT THE BUZZARDS AREN'T CIRCLING ABOVE US...

WE CAN'T EVEN HAVE A REAL BUZZARD!

THERE'S MORE TO PLAYING RIGHT FIELD THAN CHEWING GUM AND BLOWING BUBBLES!

BONK!

LIKE WHAT?

COME BACK, EVERYBODY! WE CAN STILL PLAY!

A LITTLE WATER DOESN'T HURT!

THE WAVES AREN'T THAT HIGH!

THERE AREN'T EVEN ANY WHITE CAPS!
SCHULZ

SCHULZ

THERE'S A FULL MOON TONIGHT, BIG BROTHER..
YOU SHOULD GO OUT, AND LOOK AT IT
MAYBE I WILL...THANK YOU..

HOW ABOUT AN ICE CREAM CONE, BIG BROTHER?
THAT WOULD BE VERY NICE, THANK YOU..
ONE ICE CREAM CONE COMING UP!
SCHULZ

EVERYTHING I SEE LOOKS LIKE A BASEBALL TO ME...
AND NOW MY HEAD HAS STARTED TO ITCH...I THINK I HAVE A RASH OR SOMETHING...

TURN AROUND... LET ME LOOK..

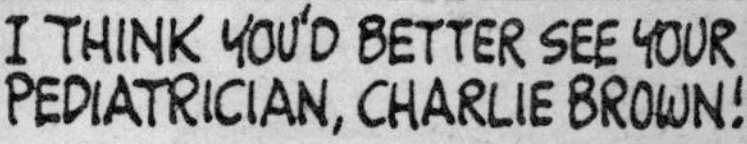
I THINK YOU'D BETTER SEE YOUR PEDIATRICIAN, CHARLIE BROWN!

SCHULZ

THIS GUY CAN'T HIT IT!

HE SWINGS LIKE MY GRANDMOTHER!

BONK!

SORRY, GRAMMA...IT WAS JUST AN EXPRESSION...
SCHULZ

WELL, I GUESS I'LL PUT THE OL' BAT AWAY FOR ANOTHER YEAR

THIS HAS BEEN A GOOD BAT...

I'VE HAD IT FOR THREE SEASONS, AND THERE ISN'T A CRACK IN IT!

TO CRACK A BAT, YOU HAVE TO HIT THE BALL!
SCHULZ

DON'T TRY TO TELL ME THAT THE SUN GOT IN YOUR EYES! OR THE MOON, EITHER! OR THE CLOUDS, OR THE SMOG OR THE CRAB GRASS!

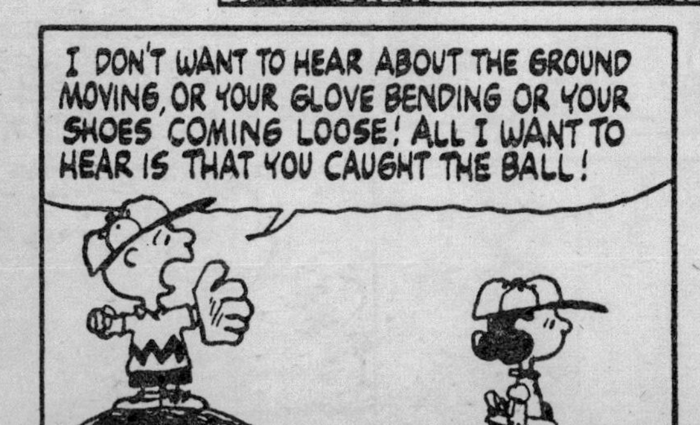

PLUNK

ACTUALLY, I WAS KIND OF LOOKING FORWARD TO A NEW EXCUSE...
SCHULZ

WHICH IS CORRECT, "WHO ARE WE KIDDING?" OR "WHOM ARE WE KIDDING?"
WELL, I SUPPOSE "WHOM" IS CORRECT ALTHOUGH MOST PEOPLE WOULD SAY "WHO"
WHAT DO YOU THINK OUR CHANCES ARE OF WINNING TODAY?

OH, I'D SAY ABOUT FIFTY-FIFTY...

WHOM ARE WE KIDDING?
SCHULZ

POW!

LOOK, CHARLIE BROWN... I CAUGHT YOUR SHOE!

MAYBE I SHOULD PITCH MY SHOE INSTEAD OF THE BALL..
THAT'S A GOOD IDEA..GIVE 'EM THE OL' KNUCKLE SHOE!
SCHULZ

"WHO SHUT IN THE SEA WITH DOORS WHEN IT BURST FORTH FROM THE WOMB? HAVE YOU ENTERED THE STOREHOUSE OF THE SNOW?"

"WHO CAN NUMBER THE CLOUDS BY WISDOM? OR WHO CAN TILT THE WATERSKINS OF THE HEAVENS?"

"IS THE WILD OX WILLING TO SERVE YOU? DO YOU GIVE THE HORSE HIS MIGHT? IS IT BY YOUR WISDOM THAT THE HAWK SOARS, AND SPREADS HIS WINGS TOWARD THE SOUTH?"

DON'T CRITICIZE THE WORLD, CHARLIE BROWN

HOW WOULD IT BE IF I JUST YELLED AT THE UMPIRE?
SCHULZ

HEY, MANAGER!

I'VE DECIDED THAT I SHOULD BE PAID A MILLION DOLLARS A YEAR

BRRATRRR!!

SO MUCH FOR ARBITRATION...
SCHULZ

YOU KNOW WHAT?
THE LAST PIANO OWNED BY BEETHOVEN HAS BEEN SENT TO NUERNBERG FOR RESTORATION
THAT'S VERY INTERESTING

MY CATCHER HAS MANY THINGS ON HIS MIND!
SCHULZ

BEFORE WE START THE GAME, CHARLIE BROWN, YOU HAVE TO ASK THE BALL IF IT WANTS TO PLAY..

I HAVE TO WHAT ?

YOU HAVE TO ASK THE BALL IF IT WANTS TO PLAY! YOU ASKED THE OTHER TEAM, DIDN'T YOU? AND YOU ASKED ALL OF YOUR OWN PLAYERS, DIDN'T YOU? OF COURSE, YOU DID!

NOW, YOU HAVE TO ASK THE BALL! AFTER ALL, THE BALL IS THE ONE WHO'S GOING TO GET HIT ALL THE TIME, ISN'T IT? DON'T YOU THINK IT SHOULD HAVE A CHOICE?

GO AHEAD, CHARLIE BROWN....ASK THE BALL.. ASK THE BALL IF IT WANTS TO PLAY...

I FEEL LIKE A FOOL

HEY, BALL..DO YOU WANT TO PLAY IN THE GAME TODAY?

IT DIDN'T ANSWER
IT'S TRYING TO MAKE UP ITS MIND...I GUESS I'LL GO HOME...

GO HOME?!
I'M NOT GOING TO STAND AROUND ALL DAY WHILE SOME STUPID BALL TRIES TO MAKE UP ITS MIND!
SCHULZ

I'M SORRY I'M LATE, CHARLIE BROWN..IS THE GAME OVER?
NOT QUITE..

I'M AFRAID IT'S ALL OVER BUT THE SHOUTING...

WE'RE BEHIND SIXTY-THREE TO NOTHING

AAUGHH!

NOW, IT'S OVER
SCHULZ